UNCOVERING HISTORY

THE ANCIENT ARAB AND ISLAMIC WORLD

First published by McRae Books
Copyright © 2003 McRae Books Srl, Florence (Italy)
Borgo Santa Croce, 8 – 50122 – Florence (Italy)
This edition published under license from McRae Books.
All rights reserved.

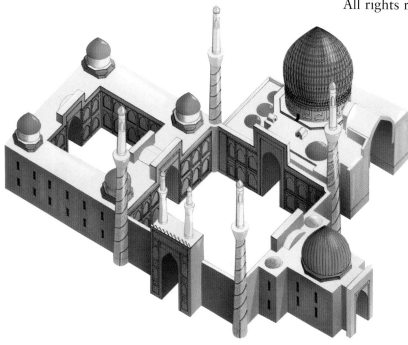

SERIES EDITOR Anne McRae
TEXT Nicola Barber
CONSULTANT Dr. Robert Hoyland
ART CONSULTANT Andrea Ricciardi di Gaudesi
ILLUSTRATIONS Manuela Cappon, Gaetano Cavotta, Giacinto Gaudenzi, Sabrina
Marconi, Lucia Mattioli, Alessandro Menchi, Paola Ravaglia, Claudia Saraceni,
Studio Stalio (Alessandro Cantucci, Fabiano Fabbrucci, Andrea Morandi)
GRAPHIC DESIGN Marco Nardi
LAYOUT Nick Leggett, Starrydog Books
EDITING Claire Moore and Anne McRae
REPRO Litocolor, Florence
PICTURE RESEARCH Claire Moore

Published in the United States by Smart Apple Media
2140 Howard Drive West, North Mankato, Minnesota 56003

U.S. publication copyright © 2006 Smart Apple Media
International copyright reserved in all countries. No part of this book may
be reproduced in any form without written permission from the publisher.
Printed and bound in Belgium

Library of Congress Cataloging-in-Publication Data

Barber, Nicola.
The ancient Arab and Islamic world / by Nicola Barber.
p. cm. — (Uncovering history)
Includes bibliographical references and index.
ISBN 1-58340-707-3
1. Arabs—History—To 622—Juvenile literature.
2. Islamic Empire—History—Juvenile literature. I. Title. II. Series.

DS38.B33 2005
909'.0976701—dc22   2004051211

9 8 7 6 5 4 3 2 1

UNCOVERING HISTORY

Nicola Barber

EVERYDAY LIFE IN THE

ANCIENT ARAB AND

ISLAMIC WORLD

Illustrations by Manuela Cappon, Gaetano Cavotta, Giacinto Gaudenzi, Sabrina Marconi, Lucia Mattioli, Alessandro Menchi, Paola Ravaglia, Claudia Saraceni, Studio Stalio (Alessandro Cantucci, Fabiano Fabbrucci, Andrea Morandi)

A⁺
Smart Apple Media

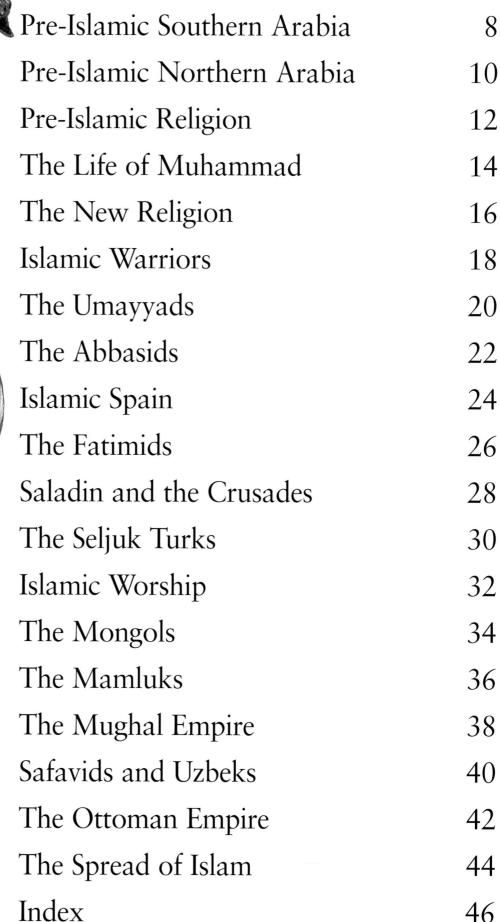

Table of Contents

Introduction

The land of Arabia is a long peninsula that stretches from the Red Sea in the west to the Persian Gulf in the east. Apart from the highlands to the south and the coastal plain to the west, it is a region of hot deserts with scattered oases. This vast land was once inhabited only by Arabs, and it was here, in the city of Mecca (Makkah), in about A.D. 570, that the Prophet Muhammad was born.

The people of Arabia worshiped many gods, but after the Prophet Muhammad received the first of his many messages from Allah (God) in about A.D. 610, he took his new religion to the most distant parts of the Arabian peninsula and into modern-day Jordan. Under his successors, the Islamic religion was taken even farther afield, spreading north into Syria, east into Mesopotamia, and west into Egypt and North Africa. By means of Islam, the Arab people were slowly released from their desert confines and taken as far away as Spain in the west and India in the east.

The success of Islam was seen in the conversion of many conquered populations to the new religion. Although all Muslims were originally Arabs, people from a huge diversity of ethnic backgrounds soon began calling themselves Muslims and eagerly contributed to the shaping of the new religion. The very fact that the earliest surviving Koranic commentary was written by a man of Persian origins, and the first Arabic grammar by a native of modern-day Afghanistan, shows us the influence and extent of the new religion.

As history progressed, non-Arab Muslim dynasties took control of many parts of the world, bringing with them their own cultures and developments. Today, the worldwide community of Muslims numbers more than one billion and is composed of people from a multitude of nationalities and ethnic backgrounds.

Chronology of the Ancient Arab and Islamic World

SEVERAL THRIVING KINGDOMS IN SOUTHERN ARABIA
500 B.C.

CITY OF PALMYA GAINS PROMINENCE
3rd century B.C.

PETRA IS ANNEXED TO ROME
106 B.C.

BIRTH OF THE PROPHET MUHAMMAD
c. A.D. 570

PROPHET MUHAMMAD RECEIVES THE FIRST REVELATION IN THE CAVE AT HIRA
610

DEATH OF THE PROPHET MUHAMMAD
632

DEATH OF THE FIRST CALIPH, ABU BAKR. UMAR BECOMES SECOND CALIPH
634

FIRST MUSLIM INVASION OF SPAIN
711

UMAYYADS ARE OVERTHROWN. ABBASIDS COME TO POWER
750

FATIMIDS CONQUER EGYPT
969

SELJUK TURKS DEFEAT BYZANTINES AT BATTLE OF MANZIKERT
1071

SALADIN ENDS FATIMID RULE IN EGYPT
1171

GHENGIS KHAN PROCLAIMED RULER OF THE MONGOLS
1206

TIMUR BECOMES RULER OF SAMARKAND
1370

BABUR FOUNDS MUGHAL EMPIRE
1526

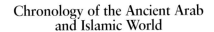

Pre-Islamic Southern Arabia

Historians of the early Arabs divide the Arabian people into those who lived in the south of the Arabian Peninsula and those who lived in the north. Southern Arabia covered the region that is modern-day Yemen and Oman. One of the earliest kingdoms named in surviving records was Saba, which may date back to the 10th century B.C. It is almost certainly the same kingdom that is called Sheba in the Bible and is also mentioned in the Koran.

A gold earring and beads from ancient southern Arabia. Gold was mined in western Arabia, and there is also evidence of gold-working in southern Arabia.

Ancient society

Society in most of pre-Islamic Arabia was structured around the tribe—a group of people strongly bound together by common ancestry and kinship. Members of a tribe protected each other in times of trouble. Southern Arabia was also divided into a number of kingdoms during ancient times, the most famous of these being Saba, with its capital at Marib. Thousands of inscriptions on stone, wood, and bronze discovered at sites in Yemen provide evidence of Saba, which flourished from the eighth century B.C., to the end of the third century B.C.

Heavily laden camels carry spices and aromatics northward through the deserts of Arabia.

This stone incense burner from southern Arabia dates from the first century B.C. Incense was a mixture of myrrh and frankincense oils.

The caravan routes

The rich goods of southern Arabia were transported by ship from the ports along the southwestern Arabian coast and by camel caravan through the deserts to the north. Laden with heavy bags of spices and aromatics, long lines of camels trudged along the dusty desert tracks. Domesticated by nomadic Arabs around 900 B.C., the camel was a strong animal, and since it stored water in its hump, it could survive for long periods without water. The use of the camel as a pack animal opened up new transportation routes.

Arabia Felix

The Ancient Romans called the region "Arabia Felix," meaning "fortunate Arabia," because of its reputation as a land of great wealth and prosperity. This reputation came from trade, particularly the export of spices and aromatics such as myrrh and frankincense. These substances were used as perfumes and medicines, as well as to make incense. A regular trade developed with Mesopotamia, Egypt, the eastern Mediterranean countries, India, and even China.

Agriculture

Farming was the basis of society in ancient southern Arabia. Rainfall is limited across Arabia, so agriculture relied on various methods of catching, storing, and distributing water. In the seventh century B.C., the Sabaeans built a large dam at Marib, which fed about 23,700 acres (9,600 ha) of irrigated fields. A wide range of crops was grown, including grains such as wheat, barley, and sorghum; vegetables; and other crops such as vines, dates, and fruits.

The kingdoms of southern Arabia—Sabaea, Qataban, Hadhramaut, and Ma'in—traded spices and incense with many different countries.

Left: Two oxen pull the plow of a Sabaean man. A good harvest was essential for survival.

Irrigation devices included dams, wells, and cisterns for the containment and storage of water and canals to carry water to the fields. Valley slopes were often terraced to prevent water from flowing away.

Pre-Islamic Northern Arabia

This coin shows the Nabatean king Aretas IV. The inscription reads "King of Nabatu, who loves his people."

The Nabateans

The Nabateans were nomads who originally lived on the borderlands of Arabia and Syria. During the fourth and fifth centuries B.C., they moved southward and began to take control of the trade routes. Their prosperity was soon based on commerce, as rich camel caravans passed through their capital, Petra, on their way from the southern Arabian kingdoms to the Mediterranean. At the height of its power, the Nabatean kingdom extended from the Gulf of Aqaba to the Dead Sea.

The Bedouin lived in easily portable tents, which provided protection from the harsh desert environment.

Northern Arabia covered modern-day Saudi Arabia, as well as parts of Jordan and Syria. It is an inhospitable region, with deserts, steppes, and mountains. Agriculture was only possible around oases. Some people lived a settled existence in these fertile areas. But most people of northern Arabia were nomadic—they moved from place to place with their herds of animals. Little is known about these early northern Arabian peoples. However, we do know of the Nabateans, who established a trade-based kingdom during the second century B.C., with its capital at Petra.

This limestone bust comes from Palmyra and dates from the second century A.D. It shows a noblewoman adorned with intricate jewelry.

Palmyra

The city of Palmyra in modern-day Syria was built around a spring and stood on one of the main routes for trade with Mesopotamia. It was under Roman control when it came to prominence in the third century A.D. Under the rule of Queen Zenobia, its armies conquered much of Asia Minor and made a bid for Rome. Emperor Aurelian, however, regained Palmyra in A.D. 272.

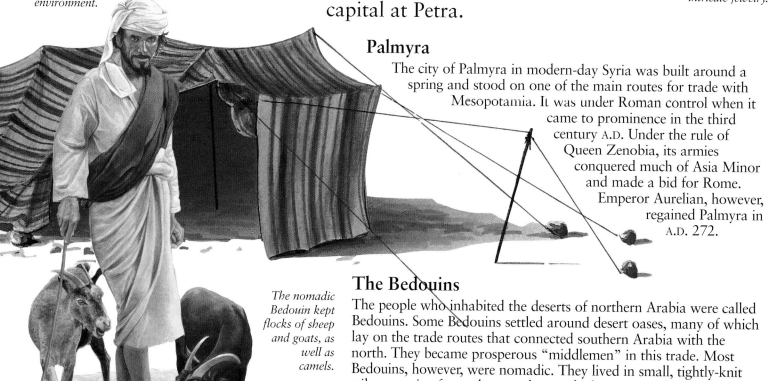

The nomadic Bedouin kept flocks of sheep and goats, as well as camels.

The Bedouins

The people who inhabited the deserts of northern Arabia were called Bedouins. Some Bedouins settled around desert oases, many of which lay on the trade routes that connected southern Arabia with the north. They became prosperous "middlemen" in this trade. Most Bedouins, however, were nomadic. They lived in small, tightly-knit tribes, moving from place to place to find water and fresh pasture and sometimes raiding neighboring states or passing camel caravans.

Traders do business, and camel caravans pass by the large, open marketplace in the center of Petra.

Petra

The ancient city of Petra, capital of the Nabateans, lies in modern-day Jordan. The city is on a plateau, surrounded by sandstone mountains through which wadis (seasonal streams) flow. The main stream provided a constant water supply for the city. The buildings of the city were cut out of mountain rock. Such buildings included temples, tombs, markets, and a theater. Their classical styles show the influence of Greek and Roman architecture and reflect the Nabateans' close links with the Roman Empire.

After the fall of the Roman Empire, the Byzantines controlled Petra (beginning in the fourth century A.D.). This mosaic decorates the floor of a large church built by the Byzantines in Petra.

Left: These blue and yellow glass pots from the fifth century B.C. were made to hold perfumes.

Pre-Islamic Religion

There is little information about religion in pre-Islamic Arabia. The evidence that has been collected comes from inscriptions, ancient poems, and ancient Greek literature. Some early Muslim scholars also collected information on pre-Islamic gods and rituals. The ancient Arabs generally believed in a powerful patron deity who ruled the universe together with various minor gods and goddesses, as well as objects such as stones and trees. They also worshiped the sun, the moon, and other heavenly bodies.

This statue represents the god Baal, the Canaanite storm and weather god.

Gods and goddesses

The ancient Arabs worshiped a wide range of gods and goddesses. The principal god of the Nabateans was Dushara, whose cult spread far beyond the borders of the Nabatean kingdom with the expansion of Nabatean trade. Well-known goddesses such as al-Lat and al-Uzza were honored along with the god Manah. The Arabs also worshiped demons and spirits, called jinn.

Some ancient Arabs also worshiped trees, as shown in this Persian illustration.

Religious practices

The ancient Arabs believed that certain places, including springs, mountain tops, caves, and patches of forest, were occupied by the gods and goddesses. These sacred areas were usually marked by a row of upright pillars. In cities, temples were often built on such sites and dedicated to a particular god or goddess, who was represented by a statue or by a sacred stone. People came to these open-air and indoor temples for rituals and ceremonies, bringing offerings, including crops and food, milk and wine, aromatics, and animals to be sacrificed.

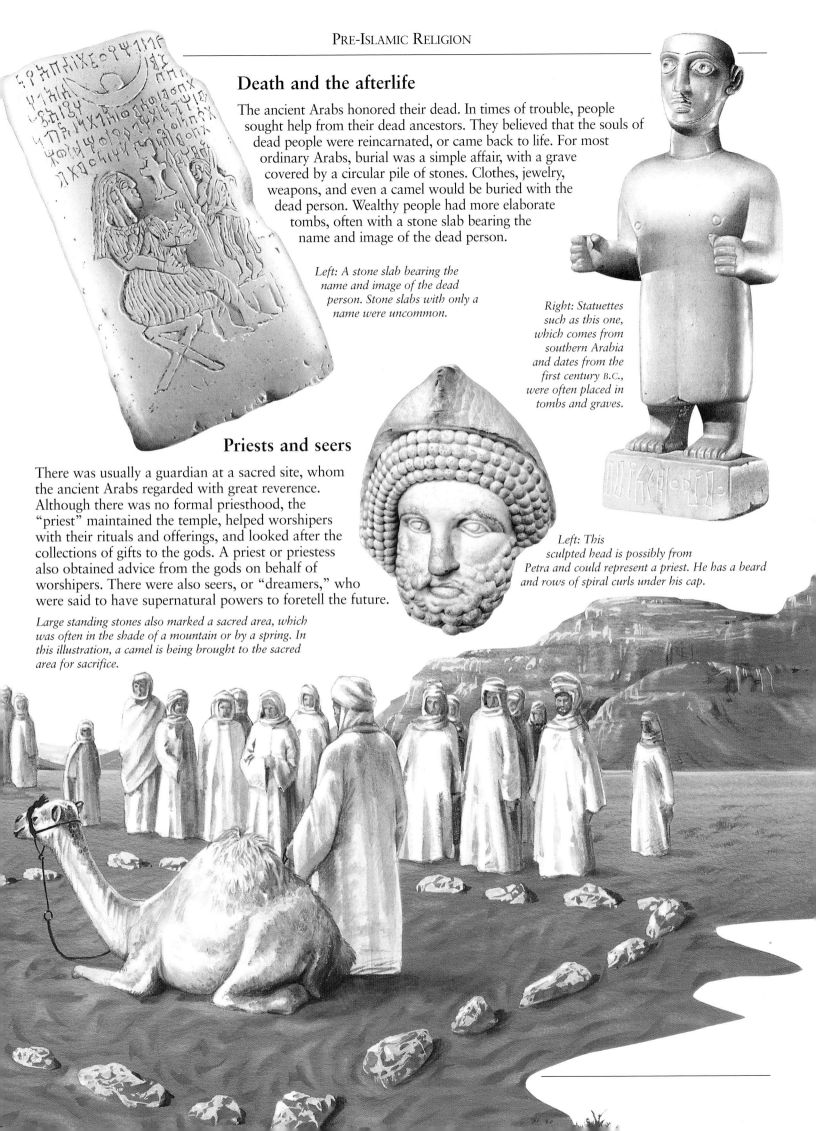

Death and the afterlife

The ancient Arabs honored their dead. In times of trouble, people sought help from their dead ancestors. They believed that the souls of dead people were reincarnated, or came back to life. For most ordinary Arabs, burial was a simple affair, with a grave covered by a circular pile of stones. Clothes, jewelry, weapons, and even a camel would be buried with the dead person. Wealthy people had more elaborate tombs, often with a stone slab bearing the name and image of the dead person.

Left: A stone slab bearing the name and image of the dead person. Stone slabs with only a name were uncommon.

Right: Statuettes such as this one, which comes from southern Arabia and dates from the first century B.C., were often placed in tombs and graves.

Priests and seers

There was usually a guardian at a sacred site, whom the ancient Arabs regarded with great reverence. Although there was no formal priesthood, the "priest" maintained the temple, helped worshipers with their rituals and offerings, and looked after the collections of gifts to the gods. A priest or priestess also obtained advice from the gods on behalf of worshipers. There were also seers, or "dreamers," who were said to have supernatural powers to foretell the future.

Left: This sculpted head is possibly from Petra and could represent a priest. He has a beard and rows of spiral curls under his cap.

Large standing stones also marked a sacred area, which was often in the shade of a mountain or by a spring. In this illustration, a camel is being brought to the sacred area for sacrifice.

The Life of Muhammad

Muhammad's early life

The prophet Muhammad was born in about A.D. 570 in Mecca, which is in modern-day Saudi Arabia. He was a member of the Quraish tribe. His father died before he was born and his mother when he was six, so Muhammad was brought up by his grandfather and his uncle, Abu Talib. Mecca was a trading center, and Muhammad worked for his uncle, who was a merchant. Muhammad married a widow, Khadijah, and they had six children.

This Ottoman miniature from the 16th century shows the birth of Muhammad.

Islam was introduced into Arabia in the seventh century A.D. by the Prophet Muhammad. Muslims believe that Muhammad was the last in a series of prophets. They also believe that Muhammad received the final and complete revelation from Allah. Muhammad taught his new religion to a small group of followers, and it quickly spread throughout the Middle East. The beginning of the Islamic calendar and of the Muslim era is marked by Muhammad's journey to Medina in A.D. 622.

The first calling

Muhammad often went to the mountains around Mecca to pray and meditate. One day in A.D. 610, the angel Gabriel (Jibril) appeared to him. The angel showed Muhammad some words, but Muhammad said that he was not a learned man and could not read them. Suddenly, Muhammad knew what the words said, and he recited them.

The angel Gabriel appeared to Muhammad at the Cave of Hira on Jabal Nur (the "Mount of Light").

The Night Journey

One night, the Prophet Muhammad was awakened from sleep by the angel Gabriel. Gabriel took Muhammad on a winged horse to Mount Zion in Jerusalem. From here, Muhammad made an ascent into Heaven, approaching the throne of Allah. He then returned to Mecca. During the night, Allah gave Muhammad the instructions about daily prayer and practice that have formed the basis of Muslim life ever since.

It is said that Muhammad saw many prophets from the past, including Jesus (Isa), Abraham (Ibrahim), and Moses (Musa), on his ascent into Heaven.

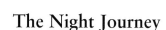

Each revelation was learned by heart and later recorded in the holy book of the Muslims, the Koran.

Muhammad's death

Muhammad and his followers made pilgrimages to Mecca in 628 and 629. His final pilgrimage was in 632. When he returned to Medina, he fell ill and was unable to lead prayers in the mosque. He died in the arms of his wife Aishah on June 8, 632.

The revelations

The words shown to Muhammad by the angel Gabriel were the first of many revelations he received during his lifetime. Sometimes, the revelations came when Muhammad was praying; at other times, they came while he was doing ordinary things in his daily life.

The Prophet Muhammad was buried in the place where he died. Today, his shrine is part of the mosque complex at Medina.

An illustration of Muhammad's house in Medina.

In Medina, Muslims constructed a place of worship and a home for the Prophet Muhammad. This was the first mosque.

Preaching

At first, Muhammad preached to his family and friends, but he later began to preach more publicly. Many people in Mecca felt threatened by the Prophet's words and began to persecute him and his followers. Some Muslims sought refuge in Ethiopia (Abyssinia). In A.D. 622, Muhammad moved with many of his followers to Yathrib, later called Medina. This migration is known as the Hijrah and is the starting point of the Muslim calendar.

Challenges to the new religion

After the death of the Prophet Muhammad, his father-in-law and closest friend, Abu Bakr, became the head of the Muslim community. He was the first caliph, meaning "successor" or "deputy." Many Muslims supported the choice of Abu Bakr, but some groups rebelled against his leadership and refused to pay the taxes that had been set up by Muhammad. Abu Bakr acted quickly to halt this rebellion by sending small armies to the main centers of opposition. The resulting battles are known as the Ridda Wars.

Abu Bakr (c. 573–634) was one of the Prophet Muhammad's oldest and closest friends and father of Muhammad's wife Aishah.

This Persian miniature shows a Muslim giving alms to a poor man.

The Ka'bah

The word Ka'bah means "cube," and this simple cube-shaped structure, made from stone blocks, became the sacred shrine of Islam. When Muhammad was young, people came to worship many different gods at the Ka'bah. In 629, Muhammad and his followers finally conquered the city of Mecca and threw all of the idols out of the Ka'bah. Today, the Ka'bah forms part of the pilgrimage, called the Hajj in Arabic (see page 33).

Meccan Muslims surround the sacred shrine of Islam, the Ka'bah.

The Dome of the Rock was completed in 691. Its circular dome rests on an octagonal base and is supported by 12 pillars and 4 piers. The outside of the dome is covered in gold leaf, and inside, it is decorated with mosaics. The arches between the pillars are also covered in mosaics, which are some of the few that survive from the original structure. The shrine was built as a place of pilgrimage rather than a place of daily worship.

❶ THE DOME IS COVERED IN PURE GOLD LEAF

❷ COLORED TILES DATING FROM THE OTTOMAN PERIOD

❸ MARBLE COVERS THE LOWER WALLS

❹ OCTAGONAL-SHAPED BUILDING

❺ ONE OF FOUR ENTRANCES

❻ HOLY ROCK

❼ THE INTERIOR OF THE DOME IS DECORATED WITH MOSAICS

❽ 12 COLUMNS AND 4 PIERS SUPPORT THE DOME

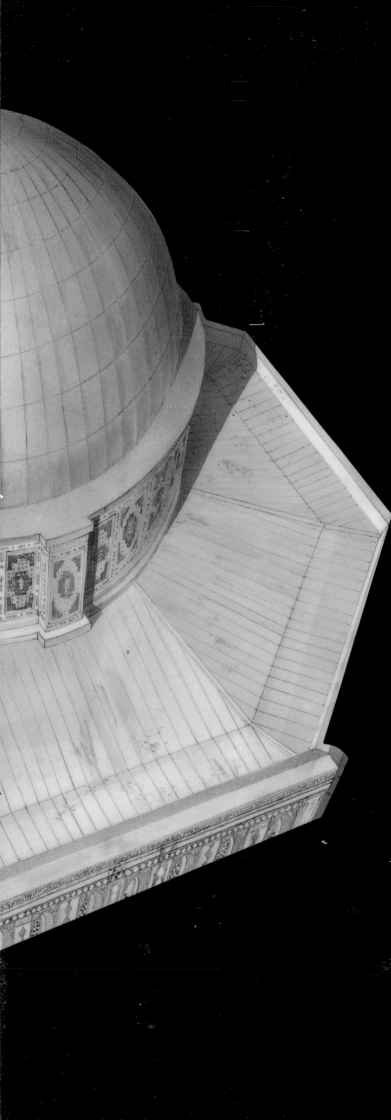

The New Religion

This brass jug was made in Basra in southern Iraq and dates from the seventh to ninth centuries—the early Islamic period.

Arabia in the seventh century A.D. was a place of many religions. Many people were Christians or Jews, and many others worshiped a variety of different gods. The Prophet Muhammad's revolutionary message was difficult for many people to accept, and during his lifetime, Muhammad endured much persecution and hardship. Nevertheless, the spread of Islam was extraordinarily rapid. By the time of Muhammad's death in A.D. 632, Islam was established in much of the Arabian peninsula, including Mecca. Over the next century, Islam continued to expand as large areas were conquered by Muslim armies.

The Dome of the Rock

Early in the Prophet Muhammad's preaching, he recognized Jerusalem, which was conquered by the Muslims in 638, as a holy city. Under the Umayyad caliph, Abd al-Malik, the Dome of the Rock was the first major Islamic monument to be built and symbolized Muslim triumph in Jerusalem. At its center was the holy rock from which Muhammad was said to have made his Night Journey.

The spread of Islam

After the death of the Prophet Muhammad, the Ridda Wars took Islam across the Arabian Peninsula, opening the way to further expansion. In many places, after initially resisting the Muslim armies, people converted to the Islamic faith. In this way, the Muslim armies swept northward and eastward through the Holy Land, Iraq and Iran, and into India, and westward across Egypt and North Africa.

ISLAM IN 632
ISLAM IN 750

The rapid spread of Islam reached its northernmost point near Tours, France, in 732, when a Muslim army was defeated there.

The conquests

At the time of Muhammad's death, the lands to the north of the Arabian Peninsula were divided between the Byzantine and Iranian empires. During the early years of the seventh century, the two empires were continuously at war with each other and were not able to withstand the Arab invasions. In 636, the Muslim armies, under the great Muslim general Khalid ibn al-Walid, defeated the Byzantines to take Syria. A year later, the Sasanian armies were also subdued, and the Arab conquerors entered Ctesiphon, the Sasanian capital (in modern-day Iraq). By the 670s, Alexandria in Byzantine Egypt and much of North Africa were under Muslim rule.

Muslim invaders reached Spain in the 700s. In this French miniature, the Muslim soldiers are portrayed as devils. Christians often used the word "infidels," meaning "unfaithful ones," to describe Muslims. The invaders established military posts in the conquered lands and imposed taxes on the conquered peoples.

Islamic Warriors

The first important battles in the history of Islam took place under Muhammad's leadership. The battles of Badr in 624 and Uhud in 625 were fought against the Meccans and were ultimately indecisive. When Muhammad finally took hold of Mecca in 630, his status as a great leader was confirmed. After his death, the first four caliphs followed the example of the Prophet and continued to expand the Islamic world alongside their faithful warriors.

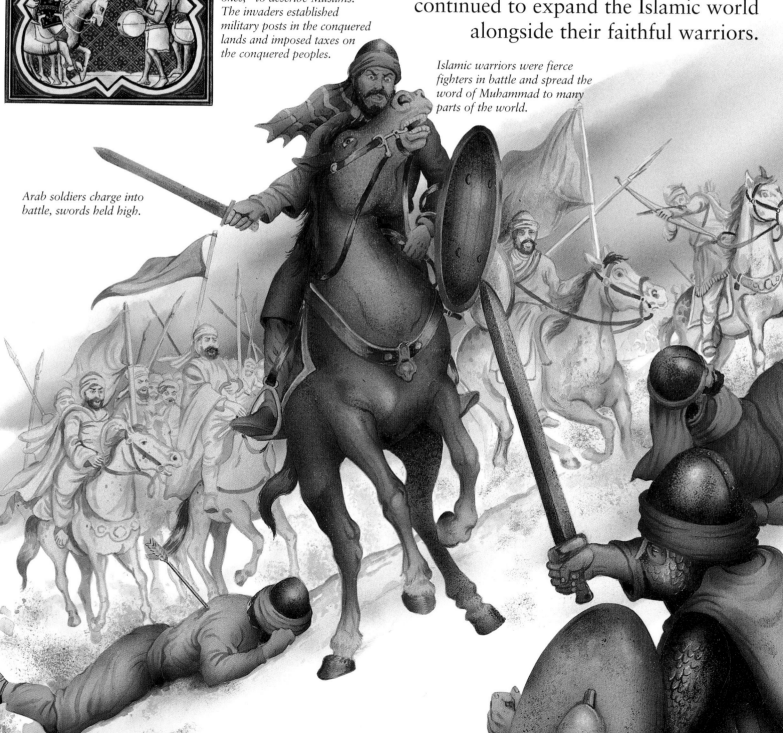

Islamic warriors were fierce fighters in battle and spread the word of Muhammad to many parts of the world.

Arab soldiers charge into battle, swords held high.

Muslim warriors

Early Muslim soldiers rode horses or camels and were armed with bows, spears, and swords. For protection, they wore coats of flexible armor and helmets and carried small, round shields. Women also had their part to play in battle, often guarding the encampments against attackers, shouting encouragement, and tending the wounds of their men.

Helmets like this were worn by Muslim warriors in battle. Muhammad wore a similar helmet in the Battle of Uhud in 625.

Battle tactics

The early Muslim soldiers were tribesmen accustomed to having to defend themselves. As a result, they were far more self-sufficient than soldiers in more conventional armies, who relied on army supplies to reach them. These Muslim soldiers were lightly armed, swift, and mobile on their horses or camels. Later, the Muslims employed professional soldiers and adopted more formal techniques of war, with drawn-up battle lines. They also learned siege techniques.

The Umayyads

The Umayyad family of the Arab tribe of Quraish was the first great dynasty of the Muslim Empire. The first Umayyad caliph, Mu'awiya, came to power in A.D. 661, after the death of the fourth caliph, Ali. The Umayyads ruled the Islamic world until A.D. 750. During this time, some of the most spectacular mosques were built, including the Dome of the Rock in Jerusalem. The high point of the dynasty was the reign of Abd al-Malik (685–705), during which the empire was extensively reorganized.

Arabs swear allegiance to Ali after the murder of the third caliph, Uthman.

Shiites believed that Husain was the rightful successor of Ali as caliph, but Husain and his family were killed by Yazid's Umayyad forces in 680 (left).

Rise to power

Although the first two caliphs enjoyed the support of the Muslim community, unrest began to grow under the leadership of the third, Uthman. Uthman was murdered in 656, and Muhammad's cousin and son-in-law, Ali, became the next caliph. His appointment sparked the first civil war (656–61). Most Muslims believed that the caliph should be the person best able to uphold the customs and traditions (the Sunnah) of Islam. These Muslims became known as Sunni. Others believed that only someone directly related to Muhammad should become caliph. These Muslims became known as Shiites, meaning belonging to the party (Shia) of Ali. At the end of the first civil war, the Umayyads seized power.

Early Umayyads in Damascus

Mu'awiya was governor of Syria for 20 years before becoming caliph in A.D. 661. He decided to make Damascus the capital of the Muslim world, and he used the well-trained soldiers of the Syrian army to continue the expansion of the Islamic Empire. He divided the empire into provinces and put loyal governors in charge. Before his death, he chose his son Yazid as the next caliph, but once again, disagreements over the succession led to civil war (684–91).

Desert palaces

During the Umayyad dynasty, the caliphs and members of the ruling families built desert palaces on the edge of settled areas in Syria, Jordan, and Palestine. It is thought that the builders of these palaces may have wanted to escape city life and diseases. The palaces were often elaborate, with living quarters, baths, a hall for entertainment, a park, and a mosque. They were richly decorated, reflecting the great wealth of the Umayyad rulers.

This bathhouse, built at a desert palace in Jordan in the 740s, had hot and cold rooms and bathrooms.

This coin shows the caliph carrying the sword of Islam, a symbol of power.

The later Umayyads

The turmoil of the second civil war came to an end during the reign of the caliph Abd al-Malik (685–705). Under his leadership, Arabic was made the official state language, new Arabic coins were introduced, and a postal service was set up between Damascus and other important towns in the empire. He was succeeded by his sons al-Walid (705–15) and al-Suleiman (715–17).

The Great Mosque had a large open courtyard, surrounded by an arcade. The hall of worship ran along the south side (the direction of Mecca) and was divided into three long aisles by rows of columns supporting arches.

Above: The walls of the Great Mosque in Damascus were covered in beautiful mosaics, such as this one from a courtyard wall.

The Great Mosque of Damascus

The Great Mosque in Damascus was built between 705 and 715 under the leadership of the Umayyad caliph, al-Walid. It was constructed on an area where the Romans had originally built a large temple dedicated to Jupiter. The temple was destroyed in 390 to make way for a Christian Byzantine basilica (church) dedicated to St. John the Baptist. In turn, the Muslims demolished the basilica to make way for the mosque, which became the pattern for many other mosques in the early Islamic world.

Building the Great Mosque of Damascus. The Muslim builders reused many elements of the older Byzantine basilica in the construction of the mosque.

The Abbasids

A band of Arabian woven silk.

This scene from The Thousand and One Nights *shows Harun al-Rashid taking a bath.*

The second great dynasty of the Muslim Empire, that of the Abbasids, came to power in 750 after defeating the last Umayyad caliph at the battle of the Great Zab River in northern Iraq. The Abbasid dynasty lasted until 1258. Under the Abbasids, the focus of the Islamic Empire moved eastward, and in 762, a new capital was founded at Baghdad (in present-day Iraq). The era of expansion also came to an end. Instead, the Abbasids promoted trade and commerce, the arts, and science across their vast empire.

Abbasid splendor

A new Islamic capital was built in Baghdad in 762. The city was built within round walls roughly 1.7 miles (2.7 km) across, and it was here that the Abbasids set up a glittering court. By the eighth century, it was considered the richest city in the world and was a center for commerce and intellectual life. The famous stories of *The Thousand and One Nights* describe the riches and excesses of the Abbasid court during the reign of the fifth Abbasid caliph, Harun al-Rashid (789–809).

Above: Scholars at work in the famous library at Baghdad.

The study of water and methods of collecting, storing, and distributing it were very important in the Islamic Empire. Water wheels such as these were used to raise water from one level to another.

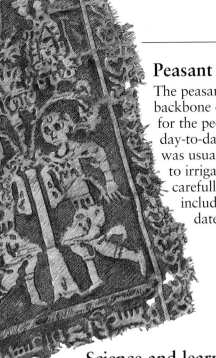

Peasant life

The peasants who worked the land formed the backbone of the Abbasid Empire, providing food for the people. But we know little about their day-to-day lives. Farming in the Islamic Empire was usually very intensive because of the need to irrigate the land and to use every part of it carefully. Many different crops were grown, including grains and fruits such as apricots, dates, and figs.

This illustration from Pseudo-Galen's Book of Antidotes *(1199) shows peasants harvesting, threshing, and winnowing grain.*

Science and learning

When Harun al-Rashid died, his two sons fought over who should succeed him. Al-Mamun eventually emerged as the next caliph. He encouraged all aspects of science and learning, setting up a grand library called the House of Wisdom. He also collected manuscripts of important works from outside the Islamic Empire for translation and study by Muslim scholars. These were collected into a famous library, which became a center of learning. Baghdad was also a center for astronomy, medicine, philosophy, literature, history, and geography.

Around 1200, the engineer al-Jazari described a range of machines in his Book of Ingenious Mechanical Devices. *This illustration (right) shows a hand washing device, in which the servant pours water from a pitcher.*

Abbasid art

The arts flourished under Abbasid rule. Fine textiles were designed for clothing and furnishings. Metal decorated with beautiful patterns often incorporated Arabic inscriptions. Everyday objects were made out of brass, but gold and silver were used for more precious items. Potters used advanced techniques, such as luster, in which glazes were painted onto items such as plates and bowls to give them a metallic sheen.

An Abbasid plate with designs painted in metallic luster.

Trade

When Al-Mansur (reigned 754–75) chose the site for his new capital, he had very practical reasons for selecting Baghdad. The city lay at an intersection of overland trade routes coming from all directions. It also had a canal linking it to the great Tigris and Euphrates Rivers. The city quickly became a center for trade and commerce, with ships unloading goods from as far away as China, India, and East Africa.

A glass bottle from the Abbasid Empire, dating back to the ninth century.

Islamic Spain

Muslim control of Spain began in the eighth century, when Berber raiders crossed the narrow straits separating the Iberian peninsula from North Africa. Umayyad rule was established in Spain in 756 by Abd al-Rahman, the only survivor of the destruction of the Umayyad dynasty in Syria. The Umayyads based themselves at Cordoba and ruled Spain until 1031. During this time, Spain became a center for intellectual and cultural life.

High-quality pottery was produced in Spain during the time of Muslim rule. This lusterware dish was made in Valencia in the early 15th century.

Arabs in Spain

After the first Muslim invasion in 711, the advance of the Muslim armies across Spain was rapid. By 718, much of Spain was under Muslim control. The rule of the Umayyad dynasty (756–1031) was followed by the Berber Almoravid and Almohad dynasties. The Christian reconquest of Spain began during the 11th century and ended in 1492, when the last Muslim stronghold, Granada, was regained.

This 19th-century engraving shows Abd al-Rahman arriving in Cordoba in 756.

Alhambra Palace

During the 11th century, Muslim Spain was attacked by Christian forces from the north and Berbers from the south. The Christian reconquest continued until the end of the 13th century, when the only remaining Muslim stronghold was Granada. The rulers of Granada lived in a fortified palace called the Alhambra, built between 1238 and 1358 on a hill overlooking the city. The high walls of the Alhambra surrounded several palaces, famed for their beautiful courtyards and gardens, as well as their intricate geometric stone carving and stucco work.

The Alhambra Palace with the Court of the Myrtles in the foreground, the Hall of the Ambassadors to the left, and beyond, the Court of the Lions, with its exquisite decorative stonework.

❶ COLONNADED ARCADE
❷ INTRICATE STONE CARVING
❸ COURT OF THE LIONS
❹ CENTRAL FOUNTAIN SURROUNDED BY 12 WHITE MARBLE LIONS

❺ ROOM OF THE ABENCERRAJES
❻ FOUNTAIN

Islamic culture

Abd al-Rahman I began the construction of the Great Mosque in Cordoba. He also started work on many other projects, including palaces, bridges, baths, and gardens. The peak of Muslim Spain came in the 10th century, under the rule of Abd al-Rahman III (912–61). By this time, Cordoba was a beautiful and civilized city. It was also an intellectual center, with many libraries, as well as a center for arts and crafts.

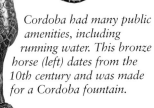

Music flourished in Cordoba, particularly under the influence of a Persian musician named Ziryab, who came to the court of Abd al-Rahman II (822–52). The lute (a small stringed instrument) is of Moorish origin, but the word "lute" comes from the Arabic al'ud.

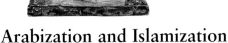

Cordoba had many public amenities, including running water. This bronze horse (left) dates from the 10th century and was made for a Cordoba fountain.

Arabization and Islamization

During the early years of the Umayyad dynasty, Muslims, Christians, and Jews lived closely together. The Muslim rulers were mostly tolerant of the Christians and Jews, but non-Muslims were taxed more heavily than Muslims. Although there was no requirement to do so, many Christians began to convert to Islam and to speak Arabic.

Muslims and non-Muslims in a 13th-century illustration of a war council in Seville.

The Fatimids

The Prophet Muhammad with his daughter Fatima and her husband, Ali. Ali was also Muhammad's cousin.

The Fatimid dynasty ruled large parts of the Islamic world from the early 10th to the late 12th centuries. The Fatimids were Shia Muslims. They took their name from Fatima, the daughter of the Prophet Muhammad and wife of the fourth caliph, Ali, from whom they claimed descent. Their aim was to oust the Abbasids, who were Sunni Muslims, from power. Based in North Africa and Sicily, the Fatimids expanded their empire eastward into Egypt and beyond, partly by military force and partly by the use of missionaries.

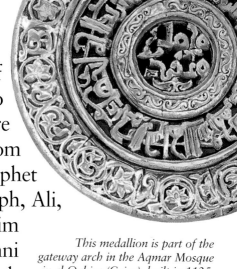

This medallion is part of the gateway arch in the Aqmar Mosque in al-Qahira (Cairo), built in 1125. At the center of the medallion is the name of Ali, the first caliph to be recognized by Shia Muslims.

The Azhar Mosque in al-Qahira (Cairo) was founded in 970–72.

Egypt—The center of power

The Fatimids came to power in northwest Africa in 909. In order to attack the strongholds of the Abbasid dynasty, they needed to expand eastward, and in 969, Fatimid troops conquered the Nile valley in Egypt. The Fatimids ruled over Egypt until 1171, building a new capital called al-Qahira (Cairo) near the old administrative center of al-Fustat. The first major building in al-Qahira was the Azhar Mosque, which also included a university that quickly became a center of Shia learning. From Egypt, the Fatimid dynasty continued to expand, taking control of Syria and parts of western Arabia during the 11th century.

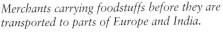

Trade and commerce

The Fatimids encouraged trade and commerce across their empire, both as a way of creating wealth and as a way of extending influence. They developed agriculture and industries in Egypt and exported Egyptian products. Major sea ports, including Alexandria and Tripoli, were under Fatimid control, and fleets of Fatimid ships sailed on the Mediterranean Sea.

Merchants carrying foodstuffs before they are transported to parts of Europe and India.

Above: This glass weight was used in the Fatimid Empire during commercial transactions.

Missionaries

The Fatimids used their armies to invade and conquer, but they also had a huge network of missionaries to threaten Abbasid power. These missionaries were trained in the centers of learning founded by the Fatimids. They were then sent into lands controlled by the Abbasids to work against the Sunni state and to convert people to Shia Islam. The Fatimids also encouraged trade, and news of Shia Islam was spread farther afield by merchants and traders.

Above: Prayer carpets like this were used in mosques throughout Cairo.

Below: A marble jug dating from 11th or 12th century Egypt.

A wall painting from a bath near Cairo, dating from the 11th century.

Fatimid art

Trade and commerce brought great wealth and luxury to the court of the Fatimids. Cairo became an important artistic center of the Islamic world, with expert craftsmen working in ivory, wood, and metal. High-quality goods, such as furniture, were also exported from Cairo throughout the Mediterranean region.

Left: This pitcher was made in Egypt during the Fatimid period and is carved from a solid piece of rock crystal. The decorative scrolls and animals are typical of Fatimid art.

Saladin (1137–93) was a great military leader.

Saladin and the Crusades

In 1169, a Kurdish military officer named Saladin (Salah al-Din) was appointed vizier (senior minister) of Fatimid Egypt. Two years later, Saladin brought Fatimid rule to an end when he proclaimed a return to Sunni Islam in Egypt. He was a skillful and wise ruler, and he encouraged scholarship and learning. Saladin also created a well-trained Muslim army to resist the advances of the Christian crusaders who, through the 12th and 13th centuries, attacked the Muslim rulers of Jerusalem and other places in the Holy Land.

The Siege of Aleppo

The citadel of Aleppo in northern Syria stands high on a hill in the center of the city. It became a focus of Muslim resistance against the crusaders in the 12th century, and from 1124 to 1125, it was besieged by the crusaders. Many different machines were used to attack a beseiged fort, including battering rams, mobile towers to lift attackers onto the ramparts, and machines to hurl rocks and other missiles. However, most sieges came to an end because of disease or lack of supplies.

The siege of Aleppo ended unsuccessfully for the crusaders. Here, a Muslim soldier fires arrows from a bow, while others fight attackers with their swords and sabers.

Muslim soldiers

Saladin's troops were quick and lightly armored. Many wore chain mail, which was much lighter than the heavy coat of mail, called a hauberk, that weighed down the crusaders. The Muslims' small horses were swift and agile compared to the larger warhorses of the crusaders. The Muslims also used various forms of communication on the battlefield, including smoke signals, fires, and messages sent by pigeon.

This Muslim warrior carries a sword and shield, an ax, and a bow and arrow.

Some crusader knights used a crossbow. It could fire farther than an ordinary bow, but it took longer to reload.

Military training often took the form of battle games, such as those in the miniature (left).

The siege of Jerusalem lasted from September 20 to October 2, 1187. It ended with surrender to Saladin and his Muslim troops. Unlike the Christian capture of the city 88 years earlier, this time there was no massacre of the inhabitants.

A crusader surrenders to Saladin after the Battle of Hattin.

Victory in Jerusalem

Saladin's greatest victories against the crusaders came in 1187. At that time, Jerusalem was under the control of the Christians. In July of 1187, Saladin's forces crushed a crusader army at Hattin in northern Palestine. After this victory, his armies swept on to Jerusalem and took the city after a short siege. The loss of Jerusalem was a crushing blow for the crusaders and sparked the Third Crusade (1189–92).

Booty from the Crusades

The crusaders plundered and stole goods wherever they went, and they often took items of great worth back home with them as souvenirs. Many of these goods became treasured parts of church collections. The crusaders also took home new ideas and tastes from their journeys to the east. These ideas, including in the area of scientific knowledge, were often far more advanced than anything known in Europe at the time. The tastes included cane sugar, citrus fruits, and spices.

This silk cloth from eastern Iran dates from the 10th century. It was brought to Europe after the First Crusade and was used to wrap precious relics in an abbey in northern France.

New foods were brought back to Europe by the crusaders.

This lion-shaped incense burner is made from metal. It dates from the 10th or 11th century and was made in Iran.

Culture and industry

The Seljuks spoke Turkish in everyday matters, but they adopted Persian as the language of their literature and culture. Under the reigns of Alp Arslan (1018–92) and his successor Malik Shah (1072–92), Seljuk art, architecture, and literature began to flourish. An extremely influential figure during this time was the Persian vizier Nizam al-Mulk. He wrote a book about government, called *Seyasat-nama*, which introduced the principles of administration. He also encouraged learning and scholarship in all fields—music, geography, science, medicine, and architecture.

This brass jug dates from the end of the 12th century. It was probably made in Herat in modern-day Afghanistan, a center for metalwork during the Seljuk period.

Tughril Beg at prayer. With his brother Chaghri, Tughril established the Seljuk Empire.

The Seljuk Turks

The Seljuks were the descendants of Turkish nomadic tribes from central Asia. They moved into Muslim-controlled territories in the late 10th century and soon converted to Sunni Islam. Under their leader, Seljuk, and his two grandsons, Chaghri Beg and Tughril Beg, they quickly conquered much of Iran and Mesopotamia (Iraq). Chaghri's son, Alp Arslan, continued the expansion of the empire with his defeat of a large Byzantine army at Manzikert in 1071. The Seljuks ruled over their empire until it finally came to an end early in the 13th century.

Seljuk architecture

Islamic architecture flourished in the Seljuk Empire, with the building of mosques, hospitals, madrasahs (Islamic schools), mausoleums (tombs), and caravanserais (lodges for merchants). The Seljuks promoted trade and safe passage for merchants traveling through their empire by building caravanserais along the main trading routes. They encouraged the study and worship of Sunni Islam by the construction of madrasahs and mosques. Under the vizier Nizam al-Mulk, Islamic architecture developed certain characteristic features, such as the conch-shaped recesses called "iwans" that faced each other in pairs across the courtyards of mosques or madrasahs.

In this scene in an Iranian tavern, musicians are playing a lute (right), a tambourine (center), and a harp (left).

The great Friday Mosque in Isfahan was built on the site of an earlier Abbasid mosque. The southern iwan (shown here) indicates the direction of prayer and is flanked by two minarets (towers).

Merchants rest at a roadside caravanserais.

*Students listen
intently to
their teachers
in a madrasah.*

*An illustration of
a Seljuk hospital.
The first hospital
was opened in
Baghdad in the
ninth century.*

Madrasahs and hospitals

Nizam al-Mulk had madrasahs
(Islamic schools) built in every major
town of the empire, with the goal of ensuring the correct teaching of
Sunni Islam. Students studied the theology and laws laid down in the Koran,
in addition to other subjects such as literature and mathematics. Many of the madrasahs
built during the Seljuk period were very elaborate, and great amounts of money were spent on their construction
since they formed such an important part of life in the Seljuk Empire. Hospitals were often built next to the
madrasahs, along with soup kitchens for the poor, dispensaries for medicines, and homes for the elderly.

Islamic Worship

Ibadah, or worship, is a very important part of a Muslim's life. Ibadah is service to Allah, and it means an awareness of Allah in all parts of everyday life. There are five special duties that every Muslim must perform; these are known as the Five Pillars. The first is Shahadah, the declaration of faith; the second is Salah, or ritual prayer, which is practiced five times a day; the third is Zakah, purification of wealth by the payment of tax; the fourth is Sawm, or fasting; and the fifth is Hajj, pilgrimage to Mecca.

The mosque

The mosque is the Muslim place of prayer. The word "mosque" originally comes from the Arabic word *masjid*, which means a "place of prostration" (a place where worshipers kneel before Allah). A mosque does not have to be a building, and in earliest times, prayers were held in houses, in the open air, and in public places. The leader of prayer in a mosque is called an imam. Inside a mosque, a decorated alcove, called a mihrab, indicates the direction of the Ka'bah in Mecca and, therefore, the direction of prayer. To the right of the mihrab is the minbar, from which the imam gives sermons on certain occasions.

The mosque usually has a large, open prayer hall covered in carpets. In the courtyard, a fountain is used for "wudu," the ritual washing that takes place before prayer.

Thirty manuscript volumes of the Koran were held in this 16th-century Ottoman box.

This open hand represents the Five Pillars of Islam. It comes from the Alhambra Palace in Granada.

Worship and belief

The daily worship practiced by Muslims today originates from the life and example of the Prophet Muhammad, known as the Sunna. Muslims learn about the Sunna in the Hadith—the sayings and teachings of the Prophet—and the Sirah—biographical writings about the Prophet. The holy book of the Muslims is the Koran. The words of the Koran were revealed to the Prophet Muhammad and form Allah's final revelation.

This 13th-century illustration shows pilgrims traveling to Mecca.

The main outer feature of a mosque is a tower called a minaret, from which a man called a muezzin calls all Muslims to prayer.

The Hajj

The fifth Pillar of Islam is the Hajj, or pilgrimage to Mecca. Every adult Muslim is required to attempt the Hajj at least once in his or her lifetime. The Hajj has been part of Muslim life since the earliest days of Islam. Every year, pilgrims from all parts of the Islamic world left their homes and traveled, sometimes vast distances, to Mecca. Muslims from many different lands were brought together during the Hajj, and this created a sense of community across the Islamic world. It also resulted in a far-flung network of communication.

Above: A burial scene from a 13th-century manuscript. Muslims paid great respect to their dead and built large cemeteries.

❶ MINARET

❷ PRAYER MATS

❸ A MAN STUDYING THE KORAN

❹ THE MOSQUE IS NOT ONLY A PLACE TO PRAY, BUT ALSO A CENTER FOR READING AND QUIET THOUGHT

❺ RITUAL PRAYER, OR SALAH, IS PERFORMED FIVE TIMES A DAY

The Mongols

The Mongols were originally nomadic tribal peoples who moved across the vast grasslands of central Asia with their flocks of sheep and goats. Early in the 13th century, the Mongol tribes united under the rule of Ghengis Khan, and the Mongol dynasty was founded. Ghengis Khan extended Mongol rule westward to Russia and eastward to northern China. At its height, the Mongol Empire included Iran, Anatolia, and Iraq. It was the first time in 600 years that a large part of the Islamic world had been ruled by a non-Muslim power.

Ghengis Khan (1162–1227). Ghengis Khan means "universal ruler."

Two Mongol warriors on horseback. Their long hair and manner of dress were copied by some Muslims after the Mongol invasions.

Military success

After being proclaimed khan (ruler) in 1206, Ghengis Khan set about training an effective and disciplined Mongol army. In 1209, the Mongols attacked and subdued Xi Xia on the northwestern border of China, then went on to China itself. The task of conquering China was completed in 1279 by Ghengis' son, Ogodei. In the west, the Mongols ran amok in Russia, Hungary, and Poland. In 1258, Mongol invaders took control of Baghdad, and the last Abbasid caliph was killed.

Right: This Mongol tunic is woven from silk and dates from the 14th century. Silk came from China, part of the Mongols' great empire.

Mongols on the move

By tradition, the Mongols were tribal nomads. During the winter, they lived in sheltered valleys, where they could graze their flocks. In the summer months, they moved to high grasslands. They lived in portable tents, called yurts, which were built on a circular framework of wooden poles and covered with thick felt or skin. The Mongols were excellent riders, breeding short, stocky horses, which were their most prized and valuable possessions.

A scene from a Mongol encampment. The Mongols were nomadic, and daily life took place wherever they set up their tents.

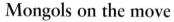
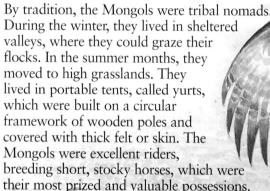
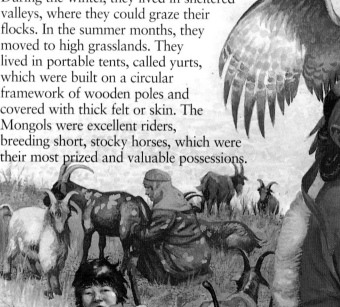

The Mongol empire

Mongol military tactics were often uncompromisingly harsh. Thousands of people were massacred, cities were looted and destroyed, and books were burned. But while the short-term effects of the Mongol invasion were undoubtedly disastrous, order and prosperity emerged once more in many areas during their rule. Many Mongols in the western part of the empire converted to Islam at the end of the 13th century. They constructed their own magnificent buildings for worship and encouraged traditions of learning.

Above: This pitcher, made from white jade, was made under the Timurids.

Above: Timur sits surrounded by the splendor and wealth of his court.

Left: A gold earring worn by a Mongol woman. Such earrings were very valuable and highly prized. Wealthy Mongol ladies wore magnificent robes made from Chinese silk. Ordinary Mongol women usually wore baggy pants.

The traditional Mongol yurt was easy to dismantle when it was time to move on. Inside, it was often furnished with colored rugs, and a brazier, or metal pan of coals, would be lit in the middle of the yurt during cold weather.

Samarkand and the Timurid dynasty

By the end of the 13th century, the huge Mongol Empire had already broken up into smaller parts. During the 14th century, under the leadership of the Muslim ruler Timur, there was one last attempt to create a united empire. Timur, who claimed to be a descendant of Ghengis Khan, made his capital at Samarkand. Here, he gathered together the finest scholars, architects, artists, and town planners to create a beautiful city. Many of the mosques, madrasahs, caravanserais, and mausoleums can still be seen today.

Below: The Gur-I Mir mausoleum in Samrkand. It is here that Timur and his descendants were buried.

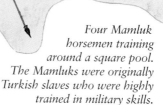

The Mamluks

The name Mamluk is an Arabic word meaning "one who is owned," or "slave," and the Mamluks were originally slaves who served in the Muslim armies. In 1250, the Mamluks overthrew the Ayyubid dynasty founded by Saladin, and the Mamluk general Baybars took control of Egypt and Syria. Mamluk rule lasted until 1517, although it is often divided into two eras. The first, known as the Bahri period, lasted until 1382 and was a time of expansion. The second era was known as the Burji period. It lasted from 1382 to 1517 and marked a gradual decline as the Ottomans rose to power.

Four Mamluk horsemen training around a square pool. The Mamluks were originally Turkish slaves who were highly trained in military skills.

Above: A scene in a tavern. Most taverns were run by Christians. Initially, the Mamluks treated Christians and Jews with tolerance, although this changed later during their rule.

Left: This jar for storing medicine dates from the 14th century.

Mamluk society

The Mamluks made their capital in Cairo and installed an Abbasid caliph there, although the caliph remained under the control of the sultan. During the Bahri period, the Mamluks fought off both the crusaders and the Mongols and ensured peace and prosperity for their empire. Cairo became a center for trade, and the Mamluks built many impressive monuments in the city. During the Burji period, the Mamluk regime became increasingly corrupt and inefficient, finally falling to the Ottomans in 1517.

Left: This brass incense burner was made in Damascus and dates from the 13th century. It is inlaid with silver and decorated with patterns and inscriptions.

Trade and the arts

The Mamluks promoted trade and commerce across their empire, and Cairo, Damascus, and Aleppo became important trading centers for goods passing between the Mediterranean and the East. Goods such as textiles, spices, and medicines were traded for wood, metals, glass, and paper. This meeting of East and West was reflected in the designs on objects such as pottery and carpets—for example, Chinese motifs such as chrysanthemums and peonies can be found on many artifacts and were incorporated into architectural decoration.

Right: A Mamluk carpet, dating from the 15th century. Cairo was famous for its carpet workshops, and carpets were exported across the Muslim world and to Europe.

A Mamluk carpet workshop. Carpets made during the Mamluk period were noted for their geometric designs.

Mamluk mosques and mausoleums

The Mamluks are renowned for the building projects they undertook in Cairo, particularly the spectacular mausoleums that dot the city. It was the custom for Mamluk sultans to build mausoleums for their own burial. In addition, they also built mosques and madrasahs. These Mamluk buildings were beautifully decorated with intricate stonework, and many of them still stand in Cairo.

Above: A mosque lamp, dating from the 14th century. It bears the name of one of the most outstanding Mamluk sultans, al-Malik an-Nasir.

Right: The dome of the mosque of Sultan Qa'itbay, built in Cairo in 1474.

The Mughal Empire

The Mughals were a Muslim dynasty that ruled over large parts of India from the 16th to the 18th centuries. They came from Afghanistan and Uzbekistan in central Asia and traced their ancestry back to Timur and Ghengis Khan. The Mughal Empire was founded in 1526 when Babur defeated the Sultan of Delhi at the Battle of Pamipal. Babur was the first of six great Mughal emperors—Babur, Humayun, Akbar, Jahangir, Shah Jahan, and Aurangzeb—who all proved themselves wise and skillful rulers. The Mughal Empire began to decline during the 18th century, coming to an end in 1858 when the British took over.

The death of Timur. This illustration comes from a history of the Timurids commissioned during the reign of Akbar.

Court life

The construction of Fatehpur Sikri, Akbar the Great's ceremonial city, began in 1571. At Fatehpur Sikri, Akbar surrounded himself with poets, painters, and musicians and encouraged religious debate between scholars of all faiths. The daily routine at court started with morning meetings in which government business was attended to. A large drum was beaten to announce the arrival of the emperor. In the afternoons and evenings, the emperor received visiting dignitaries or was entertained by events such as poetry readings or elephant fights.

A scene at the Mughal court. Akbar the Great maintained a luxurious court in which ceremony played a major daily role.

Mongol descent

The first Mughal emperor, Babur (1483–1530), claimed descent from Timur (through his father) and Ghengis Khan (through his mother). The Mughals were extremely proud of this lineage. Like his ancestors, Babur was a brilliant soldier. He led a successful campaign to capture Timur's old capital, Samarkand, when he was only 13 years old. However, he lost control of the city after only three months and spent many years trying to recapture it without success.

Above: Akbar the Great was the grandson of Babur and is considered to have been the greatest of all the Mughal emperors.

Right: Music was an important part of social life for Mughals of all classes. At events such as weddings and festivals, people sang, danced, and played musical instruments, such as trumpets, drums, and tambourines.

Left: A Mughal turban ornament decorated with precious stones.

Akbar the Great

Akbar the Great became emperor at the age of 13 and quickly took control of his empire, extending its boundaries throughout his reign. He was ruthless in putting down attacks on his power but tolerant of the other religious faiths in India, particularly Hinduism. He built a new capital at Fatehpur Sikri, near Agra, and reorganized the administration of his vast empire, dividing it into provinces and putting a governor in charge of each one.

Above: This jar dates from about 1700. It was made by Mughal craftsmen using a technique probably learned from European sources.

Artistic patrons

The arts flourished under the patronage of the Mughal emperors. One area of particular interest for Akbar and his son Jahangir was painting. Many of the paintings undertaken by artists in Akbar's court were exquisite miniatures used to illustrate books such as the *Akbar-nama*—a history of Akbar's reign. The art of miniature painting reached its height during the reign of Jahangir, with paintings of animals and birds and hunting scenes depicting the emperor and his courtiers.

Right: This hunting jacket, embroidered with floral designs, belonged to the Mughal emperor Jahangir.

This Mughal artisan is pounding paper in preparation for painting. The Mughals loved books and constructed great libraries of exquisite manuscripts. Although the language of the Mughals was Turkish, their literature was written in Persian.

Mughal architecture

Akbar's capital, Fatehpur Sikri, is only one of the Mughal architectural treasures that still stands today. The Mughal emperors built magnificent forts and palaces and huge monumental tombs. The construction of these buildings glorified the emperor and displayed his absolute power and wealth to the world. Probably the most famous of all Mughal monuments is the Taj Mahal in Agra, built by Shah Jahan for his wife Mumtaz.

The Taj Mahal is made from white marble. Construction began in 1632.

The private audience hall in Akbar's Fatehpur Sikri palace complex.

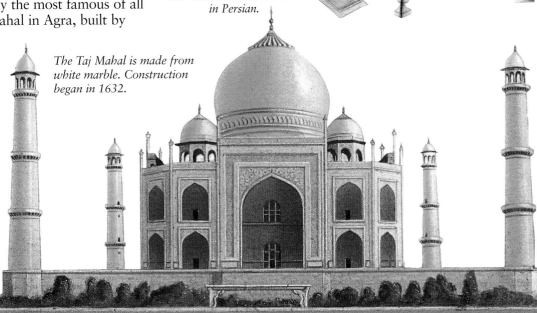

Safavids and Uzbeks

The Safavids came from Azerbaijan and got their name from their 14th-century ancestor, Safi al-Din, leader of an order of Sufi dervishes, or holy men. The Safavid dynasty was founded in 1501 by Ismail I, who extended control over territories in present-day Iran. The Safavids were Shia Muslims, and they made Shia Islam the state religion of their empire. The Safavid dynasty reached its peak under Abbas the Great (1588–1628).

❶ BAZAARS WERE COVERED WITH A ROOF
❷ THERE WERE MANY ARCHWAYS AND PASSAGES INSIDE THE BAZAAR
❸ STALL
❹ CARPETS AND SILKS WERE SOLD INSIDE THE BAZAAR
❺ WORKSHOP

Isfahan

In about 1597, Abbas the Great decided to move the capital of the Safavid Empire to Isfahan. There he built a new city, a task that took many decades and that employed many thousands of builders and craftsmen. At the center of the city was a huge rectangular public space, which was the site for markets, executions, and sports such as polo. On one side of the square stood the Lutfallah mosque, on another, the royal mosque, and on the west side, the royal palace. A huge arch marked the entrance to the covered bazaar.

Abbas the Great.

This helmet belonged to Abbas the Great. It was made from steel and gold, with an adjustable nose piece and fine mesh to protect the face and neck.

A jeweler, a pharmacist, a butcher, and a baker in a 13th-century covered bazaar.

Bazaars and trading centers

The huge bazaars at cities such as Isfahan and Bukhara had roofs for protection against the hot sun. Inside, there were stalls and workshops, and many bazaars had different areas for different types of goods—spices, cotton, silks, carpets, leather goods, food, jewelry, and metal goods. During the day, the bazaar was bustling and noisy, but it was strictly regulated by officials who made sure that traders used standard measures and maintained the quality of their goods.

Spinning the thread to be made into a carpet. Carpets were made from knotted wool, cotton, or silk.

❷

The Uzbeks

The Uzbeks traced their ancestry back to Timur and Ghengis Khan. In the 15th century, under Abul-Khayr, the Uzbeks formed their tribes into a confederation. They began to move southeast, and under the leadership of Abul-Khayr's grandson, Muhammad Shaybani, they conquered Samarkand and Bukhara at the beginning of the 16th century. The Shaybanid dynasty made its capital at Bukhara, where it built many beautiful mosques. In the 17th century, the Uzbek confederation split into three separate khanates (areas ruled by a khan): Bukhara, Khiva, and Kokand.

The Uzbeks fought with the Mughals for control over Samarkand. This illustration shows Babur entering Samarkand in 1500. However, the Uzbeks soon drove him out again.

Abbas the Great imported Ming vases and other pottery from China to teach his Persian craftsmen a new style.

Persian art

Isfahan became the center for artistic life in the Safavid Empire. Many workshops were set up in the city, and carpet weaving became very important. Most carpets were made from wool, or sometimes cotton, but very fine carpets were woven from silk. They were decorated with designs such as flowers, animals, and birds. Other workshops produced metalwork, glass, and fine pottery, often influenced by the blue and white designs of Chinese Ming pottery.

The Ottoman Empire

The Ottomans were Turkish tribes who came from central Asia and settled in Anatolia (modern Turkey). During the 14th century, they began to conquer neighboring provinces. This expansion continued throughout the 15th century, and in 1453, the Ottomans captured Constantinople and made it the capital of their empire. The Ottoman Empire reached its peak under the rule of Sultan Suleiman I but began to decline after his death. It finally came to an end in 1922.

The Janissaries were troops of the Ottoman army. Some were prisoners of war or slaves; others came from Christian peasant families. They were loyal to the sultan.

Suleiman the Magnificent

The Ottomans took their name from their first leader, Osman (also called Uthman), who founded the dynasty in about 1300. Osman's successors continued the expansion of the empire, and under Suleiman I, the empire became the largest and most powerful empire in the world. The Ottomans relied on their well-trained army, particularly the highly respected Janissaries—slaves and prisoners of war who converted to Islam. Suleiman used these troops to conquer Hungary and large parts of northern Africa. He was called "the Magnificent" by Europeans, who were stunned by the wealth and power of his court.

Suleiman the Magnificent (ruled 1520–66). He was a brilliant soldier and administrator and a patron of art and literature.

Below: Law and order were severely enforced under Ottoman rule. This man is being beaten because he has failed to keep the street clean in front of his house.

Topkapi Palace

The Ottoman court was based at the Topkapi Palace in Constantinople. The palace covered an area of 22 acres (9 ha). It was made up of many courtyards, some of which were designed for official receptions and festivities, and others of which were closed off to allow the sultan and the women of the court (the harem) to live in great privacy.

Above: A courtyard in the Topkapi Palace. The palace was the home of the sultan and his court, and beginning in the 16th century, it was the governmental seat of the Ottoman Empire.

Life in Ottoman society

The Ottomans centralized control of their huge empire, and under Suleiman I, the entire legal system was revised. Everyone in the empire was taxed, and tax records were meticulously kept. The empire was a multi-religious one, and the Ottomans were tolerant of their Christian and Jewish subjects. Men wore different colored turbans according to their religion—white for Muslims, yellow for Jews, and blue for Christians.

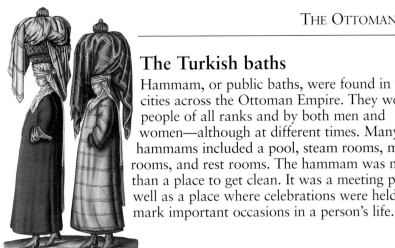

The Turkish baths

Hammam, or public baths, were found in towns and cities across the Ottoman Empire. They were used by people of all ranks and by both men and women—although at different times. Many hammams included a pool, steam rooms, massage rooms, and rest rooms. The hammam was more than a place to get clean. It was a meeting place, as well as a place where celebrations were held to mark important occasions in a person's life.

Above: Two slaves carry their mistress's belongings to the hammam. The equipment needed in a hammam included towels, wooden clogs, a bowl for pouring water, soap, a rough mitt for massage, and a jewelry box to keep the mistress's jewelry safe as she undressed. Below: the scene inside the hammam.

Ottoman arts

The Ottomans were great patrons of the arts. In Constantinople, they constructed many fine buildings, one of the most notable being the Süleimaniye Mosque. This was designed by the great architect Sinan and built during the reign of Suleiman I. Suleiman also encouraged developments in other arts, including calligraphy, painting, pottery, and carpet weaving.

Right: A mosque lamp, made during the reign of Suleiman I.

Muslims from Uzbekistan pray at a mosque.

The Spread of Islam

Islam began in the Middle East as the religion of the ancient Arabs. It quickly spread to people of other nationalities and faiths, who became Muslims. Today, it is a worldwide faith, with more than one billion Muslims forming a vast ummah, or community. Only about 20 percent of this number is of Arabic origin. In Africa, Islam originally spread across the northern part of the continent. It was carried southward across the Sahara by traders and by Muslim merchants working their way down the east coast. Islam was taken to the East by traders crossing the Indian Ocean and by merchants on long overland routes, such as the Silk Road to China.

These prayer beads come from western Sudan in Africa. They are a souvenir of one pilgrim's Hajj to Mecca.

Islam in Africa

As the word of Islam spread across West Africa, the new religion was often adopted alongside the traditional, local religions. In the 11th century, the Almoravids, under their leader Abu-Bakr, conquered much of Morocco in northwest Africa and attempted to bring the strict observance of Islamic law to their subjects. They, in turn, were taken over by the Almohads in the 12th century. During this time, the spread of scholarship and the study of the Koran spread throughout the African Muslim world. As Islam continued to spread, it was often adopted by rulers of a state or kingdom, while their subjects continued their traditional worship.

	0–1
	1–5
	5–20
	20–50
	50–90
	90–100

Today, the Islamic community stretches to most parts of the world. The map (above) shows the percentages of Muslim populations across the world. The greatest number of Muslims are in Indonesia, and large populations can be found in Pakistan, India, and Africa. There are also significant numbers in Western Europe and in the Americas, where Islamic traditions are still strongly adhered to.

Islam in the East

While Islam was spread by war and invasion across the lands close to Arabia, word of the new religion was carried by traders to more far-flung territories. In Java, Indonesia, for example, the arrival of Islam is credited to nine "wali," or teachers. In the East, Islamic influence was gradually seen in everyday life and in the arts. Javanese puppet shows, for example, began to include Islamic stories in their repertoires.

A traditional Javanese shadow puppet of Sunan Bonang, one of the nine wali.

A Chinese Muslim family celebrates the end of Ramadan. This festival, called Id-ul-Fitr, lasts for three days and is a time for feasting. People send cards with the message Id Mubarak *("Happy Feast-time") and attend the mosque for special prayers.*

To celebrate the completion of the Hajj, Muslims paint images of the Ka'bah on their houses.

Above: During the 19th century, after going on the Hajj, some Indonesian pilgrims adopted a more Arabic style of dress. Although the link between Muslim and Arab is now fairly weak, many Muslims still try to learn some Arabic and adopt an Arab name.

Celebrating Islamic festivals

Around the world, the community of Muslims celebrates the same festivals. The two most important are Id-ul-Fitr, the celebration of the breaking of the fast on the day Ramadan ends, and Id-ul-Adha, the celebration of sacrifice during the Hajj. These are the two obligatory festivals of Islam, but Muslims celebrate other days as well. Ramadan is the ninth month of the Muslim year, and the fourth pillar of Islam is observed during this month—Sawm, or fasting. Throughout this month, Muslims around the world do not touch food or drink during the day.

Index